From the Heart *of a* Father

WILLIAM JOHNSON

From the
Heart
of a
Father

**Before Our Tomorrows
Become Yesterdays**

*Inspirational Stories,
Letters of Love,
and Motivational Messages*

WILLIAM JOHNSON

SunCreek

B O O K S
Allen, Texas

ACKNOWLEDGMENTS

The stories contained in this book are not all mine. Many of them are available through a variety of sources or on the Internet and their origins are unknown or not clear. I collect them here with the purpose of complementing the letters to my sons with the inspirational messages they contain.

"Brown Paper Bag" by Robert Fulghum is reprinted from *It Was on Fire When I Lay Down on It,* copyright 1988, 1989 Robert Fulghum. Used by permission of Villard Books, a division of Random House, Inc.

Send all inquiries to:
SunCreek Books
An RCL Company
200 East Bethany Drive
Allen, Texas 75002-3804

Telephone: 800-264-0368 / 972-390-6300
Fax: 800-688-8356 / 972-390-6560

E-mail: **cservice@rcl-enterprises.com**
Website: **www.ThomasMore.com**

Printed in the United States of America

Library of Congress Catalog Number: 2002109632

5704   ISBN 932057-04-8

1 2 3 4 5   07 06 05 04 03

*To my wife Sara
and our three sons.
I am thankful for each day
we get to spend together.*

*To my parents.
Through the years when you thought
I wasn't looking, I was looking.
Thanks for being good examples
and instilling lifelong values in me.*

God took the strength of a mountain,
The majesty of a tree,
The warmth of a summer sun,
The calm of a quiet sea,
The generous soul of nature,
The comforting arm of night,
The wisdom of the ages,
The power of the eagle's flight,
The joy of a morning in spring,
The faith of a mustard seed,
The patience of eternity,
The depth of a family need,
Then God combined these qualities,
When there was nothing more to add,
He knew His masterpiece was complete,
And so, He called it . . . Dad

"IN THIS INSPIRATIONAL collection of stories and letters, Bill Johnson probes the meaning of marriage, family, and the spiritual journey. With sincerity and style, he speaks of the tender bonds that unite parents with their children and children with their parents. In a culture that often loses a sense of the primacy of family through narrow careerism and hollow achievement, this book speaks about issues that ultimately matter and values that ultimately endure. By searching his own soul for 'golden nuggets' of parental truth, Johnson offers a practical wisdom to all who are interested in growing in grace and understanding and in living by way of the heart."

—Rev. Dan Groody,
Faculty, Notre Dame University

"IN A SOCIETY that often implies that children are a burden, Bill Johnson's heartfelt letters and stories in *From the Heart of a Father* remind us that our children are gifts in our lives—gifts to be treasured each and every day. Parents will be inspired to give extra hugs and kisses to their children after reading *From the Heart of a Father.*"

—Catherine Garcia-Prats,
Mother of ten boys,
Author *(Good Families Don't Just Happen, Good Marriages Don't Just Happen)*

Contents

Introduction

THIS BOOK is about *how* I wish to be remembered by my children. If my life were to end today, would my children know my true feelings for them? Have I communicated to them what they mean to me and how important they are in my life? Do they understand the depth of my love for them? Have I communicated to my children a clear message of what values and virtues I hope to instill in them?

I hope that by sharing the personal "letters of love" I have written to my three young sons, which are "wrapped" around fictional inspirational stories, everyone who reads this book will walk away with an uplifting perspective on life.

Have I not only preached a message of faith, hope, humility, generosity, perseverance, and charity, but have I also lived it? As a friend once told me, you can't attend church on Sunday and go about your business the rest of the week as if you don't know who God is. I have to show my children on a daily basis the "love of God." I should be measured by what I do on Monday through Saturday as well as on Sunday. It is my job, as a parent, to put my words into action. I need to be a living example for my sons how I hope they live their lives.

Now, have I been a positive living example for my sons every hour of the day? Absolutely not. Have I chastised them for some event that loomed far too large in my own mind? Regretfully, I have. We all fall down. Whether that falling down is raising our voice too often or not being patient enough at times, there is always some room for improvement. And, at any particular time, if I feel that God is far away, I need to ask myself, "Who moved?" Although it's easier said than done at times, we need to pick ourselves up, we need to keep trying. We all have daily struggles. There is no shame in falling. As you pick yourself up, though, remember the outstretched hand of the One who longs to walk alongside each of us.

I have had the real blessing of being a stay-at-home dad for much of this past year. My wife was the primary caregiver for all of our sons' young lives, but she went back into the workplace when the company I was working for was downsized. The long list of "thanks, but no thanks," along with some of the negative responses I received from potential employers, made me stop and think, "Is God trying to send me a message?" Maybe staying at home to influence our sons is where I should be, for now. If we used some of the money we had in our savings and watched our spending even closer, I could stay with the boys while I looked for a new job. So this is what we have done. It has been, the saying goes, a real blessing in disguise.

The more time I spend with them, the more I realize how fast time goes by. I have always tried to spend a good deal of time with my sons, but the situation I was thrust into allowed me to spend even more time with them, doing different things. It has been a real joy and blessing to be with them when they get up in the morning, leave for school, come home in the afternoon, and, as always, to put them into bed at night.

For any of you, particularly those who might, at times, find life too busy or burdensome, I hope that you might be reenergized by reading these pages, and that your children might someday hear the words you carry in your heart. In our busy lives, too often, important things are left unsaid and our children do not hear what we may think they already know.

The idea to put my thoughts down in the form of "love letters" was partially conceived because of a regret. My maternal grandfather died suddenly when my mother was only seven and a half years old (My oldest son is now seven and a half years old.) My mother has told me many times of her sadness in losing her father at such a young age. Her sorrow in having so very little with which to really know him and remember him by still bothers her to this day. Although she remembers him as a gentle man who loved her, other than a few pictures and some birthday cards, she has nothing else.

I believe the letters of love to my three young sons, along with the inspirational stories and motivational quotes, reveal the things that are truly important in life.

For better or worse, God puts us all in each other's lives to impact one another in some way. I always tried to encourage my sons to look for God in others. Remember that no matter what happens in your life, God is always waiting for you with open arms. What a beautiful image of our heavenly Father longing for us, waiting with outstretched arms, always ready to welcome us home.

I want my children to remember me as someone who was loving, fun, firm, but fair. I want them to always feel the love I have for them. I want them to remember me as someone who, above all else, appreciated spending time with them and hopefully instilled some important values in their lives.

I hope that I will live to see my children's children. But, since none of us knows what tomorrow holds, I feel it is important to express my feelings to my children *today!*

Along with these stories I have included some "Rules for Kids," "Cheap Gifts," some humorous quotes from children about how they talk to God, and some signs on the "highway to heaven." I hope you find these simple, but sometimes profound ideas to be of great use in your daily life.

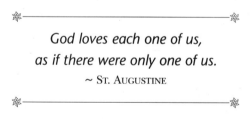

God loves each one of us,
as if there were only one of us.
~ St. Augustine

Dear Christopher, Michael, and Andrew,

The days that each of you were born had to be three of the happiest days of my life, along with the day that I married Mom. The emotion that overcame me when I finally met you face-to-face for the first time is a memory that will last a lifetime. My reaction to your births was the same—tears of joy as I realized that I had a son. What a blessing to be in the room when you were born. The most beautiful things I have ever seen were each of your newborn faces as we looked at each other for the first time.

I have known since the day each of you were born that I wanted to spend as much time with you as possible. I have always appreciated the time that I have been able to spend with you. I consider myself truly blessed for all the things that we are able to do together.

You all seem to appreciate the simple things that we do as a family. Whether it is going to the park, taking a walk, or just playing some of our favorite games inside the house, we always enjoy being together.

As you know, I have never been one to stay at the office very late. I do believe in working hard and being able to provide for our family. But, I am also a firm believer in having a family for which to provide. I think it is too great a sacrifice to work long hours at the office, insisting that it is only temporary. Before I know it, the three of you will be grown with entirely different sets of interests.

It's critical for me to spend time with you. I can't allow myself to do what others see as "important" rather than spend time with the three of you, the ones who mean the most to me. I do not get overly consumed with leaving my mark, my legacy, on the world. What does consume me is leaving my mark on the three of you, to instill in you lifelong values about faith, compassion, generosity, and family.

It saddens me to read or hear about a father who doesn't see his children growing up because he has made a choice to spend too much time away from them. The reality is that when I'm dead and gone, the job that I was doing will be filled by someone else. I am the only dad that the three of you will ever have. I value that title more than any that I might receive in the business world. You are three wonderful gifts to me.

I recently read an article about the time fathers who have sons spend at work. These fathers tend to spend more hours at work than fathers who don't have sons. After pondering this briefly, my feeling is that the reverse should be true. We need each other in our lives. We need to spend time together. Work hard at whatever you choose to do in life; just don't let it consume you. Be passionate about what you do, but be just as passionate about what's truly important in life.

The years that you all are willing to hold my hand as we cross the street, have me put you up on my shoulders, or hold you in my grasp go by incredibly fast. The innocent "I love you's" and the nights that I carry you up to bed, already fast asleep in my arms, are memories that are priceless to me. No one could ever convince me to trade more hours away from you and sacrifice these few short years with you. Each day my simple wish is to spend at least one more day with you. I am truly appreciative of the time that we are able to spend together.

Just the other day I was telling Mom that in nine short years Christopher will be thinking of going away to college. Even as I put these thoughts down on paper, that image, the one of us dropping you off at college for the first time, leaves an empty feeling inside of me. We are certainly happy, though, to watch you all grow from young toddlers into boys, and on into adulthood. I realize that I have been blessed to recognize how fast time goes by.

Someone once told me to think about what you want said at your eulogy and then live your life accordingly. Well, here's what I hope can be said on that day: "He loved God, and he loved being a husband and father. He loved his children deeply. He loved being a son and brother to his family. He knew that hard work had its place in life but, for the most part, he did not let it consume him and take him away from what he valued most, his faith and family. He realized how blessed he was to live in such a rich country in which so many of the things we take for granted are luxuries in other parts of the world. He always believed that God will provide for those who seek His help."

I hope that I leave you with three thoughts as well. First, know that faith is a central part of my life. God is so good to us and His love is unconditional. He knows the entire story of our lives but loves us more than our mind or heart could ever imagine.

Although so much love in this world is conditional, the love I have for you is not. You are my sons. I will always love you for this reason alone. If I can love the three of you, with all my imperfections, think how much more God cares for and loves each of you.

Second, I love mom and see her as a real blessing in my life. As Monsignor McMurtrie once told me: "The greatest gift a father can give to his children is to love their mother." I am blessed to have found that someone to love.

Finally, know that I am proud to walk alongside each of you in life and to be able to call you "Son." The depth of my love for you is impossible to measure. I need each of you in my life. I love you more than life itself and, like any parent, would sacrifice my life for yours in a moment.

The stories and letters that follow are meant to inspire you and leave you with lasting memories of the joy I have in being your dad.

I love you,
Dad

Success is not defined
by obtaining everything you want,
but by appreciating everything you have.

~ ANONYMOUS

The Cracked Pot

A WATER BEARER in India had two large pots, each hung on opposite ends of a pole, which he carried across his neck. One of the pots had a crack in it, and while the other pot was perfect and always delivered a full portion of water at the end of the long walk from the stream to the master's house, the cracked pot arrived only half full. For two whole years this went on daily, with the bearer delivering only one and a half pots full of water to his master's house. Of course, the perfect pot was proud of its accomplishments, perfect to the end for which it was made. But the poor cracked pot was ashamed of its own imperfection, and miserable that it was able to accomplish only half of what it had been made to do.

After two years of what it perceived to be a bitter failure, the cracked pot spoke to the water bearer one day by the stream. "I am ashamed of myself, and I want to apologize to you."

"Why?" asked the bearer. "What are you ashamed of?"

"I have been able, for these past two years, to deliver only half my load because this crack in my side causes water to leak out all the way back to your master's house. Because of my flaws, you have to do all of this work, and you don't get full value from your efforts," the pot said.

The water bearer felt sorry for the old cracked pot, and in his compassion he said, "As we return to the master's house, I want you to notice the beautiful flowers along the path."

Indeed, as they went up the hill, the old cracked pot took notice of the sun arming the beautiful wildflowers on the side of the path, and this cheered it some. But at the end of the trail, it still felt bad because it had leaked out half its load, and so again it apologized to the bearer for its failure.

The bearer said to the pot, "Did you notice that there were flowers only on your side of the path, but not on the other pot's side? That's because I have always known about your flaw, and I took advantage of it. I planted flower seeds on your side of the path, and every day while we walk back from the stream, you've watered them. For two years I have been able to pick these beautiful flowers to decorate my master's table. Without you being just the way you are, he would not have this beauty to grace his house."

Each of us has our own unique flaws. We are all cracked pots. If we will allow it, the Lord will use our flaws to grace His Father's table. In God's great economy, nothing goes to waste. So as we seek ways to minister together, and as God calls you to the tasks He has appointed for you, don't be afraid of your flaws. Acknowledge them, and allow Him to take advantage of them, and you, too, can be the cause of beauty in His pathway.

Go out boldly,
knowing that in our weakness we find His strength,
and that in Him every one of God's promises is a Yes.

~ AUTHOR UNKNOWN

Dear Christopher,

You were into the first few months of kindergarten and you were already experiencing a touch of reality. It is a shame it has to start so young, but part of our job as parents is to help you prepare and cope with things that are, for the most part, beyond our control. You were riding home on the bus one day and a few of the kids started teasing you about your height.

As you know now, no one in our family is very tall and you, being a child of ours are pretty much in the same mold. After some talks with mom and me, we were able to work through the fact that sometimes kids at any age tease those who appear different from them. We talked about how God loves us for what we are on the inside and how much more important it is to be a good person than to worry about one's physical characteristics.

We also encouraged you to get involved in some other activities outside of school. You started to show, at a very young age, a real liking to baseball. You have come to play baseball almost on a daily basis. Whether playing catch by yourself, taking batting practice with me, or the two of us playing catch, you just can't seem to get enough of it.

The fact that you are smaller than the other kids your age has given you, I believe, more determination than ever to be successful at baseball. I have seen quite an improvement since you were four years old hitting that ball off of a batting tee. Your perseverance in practicing these skills is something that you should be proud of as I am proud of you. You may not realize it at your young age, but you took a potentially negative situation and turned it into something positive. Your lack of height, which some perceived to be a weakness, you turned into a strength.

There is a bigger message that you can carry through life as you stand up to the plate and take a swing. As I have told you at different times, "take a hack at it." You can't get a hit if you don't take a chance and swing. So it is with life. Take a chance on the reasonably good situations in life (the good pitches). You're going to miss some completely (the strikes), but I bet you'll get a few hits as well. Be prepared; be confident.

I love you just as you are. God creates us in his likeness and image. God knows what our weaknesses are. He is always there to help us. He is the ultimate coach. He will put us in the proper position to be successful if we let Him.

I love you,
Dad

The person who says it cannot be done should not interrupt the person doing it.

~ CHINESE PROVERB

The Cocoon

A MAN FOUND a cocoon of a butterfly. One day a small opening appeared, and the man sat and watched the butterfly for several hours as it struggled to force its body through that little hole.

Then it seemed to stop making any progress. It appeared as if it had gotten as far as it could and it could go no farther. So the man decided to help the butterfly. He took a pair of scissors and snipped off the remaining bit of the cocoon. The butterfly then emerged easily. But it had a swollen body and small, shriveled wings. The man continued to watch the butterfly because he expected that, at any moment, the wings would enlarge and expand to support the body, which would contract in time.

Neither happened! In fact, the butterfly spent the rest of its life crawling around with a swollen body and shriveled wings. It never was able to fly.

What the man in his kindness and haste did not understand was that the restricting cocoon and the struggle required for the butterfly to get through the tiny opening were God's way of forcing fluid from the body of the butterfly into its wings so that it would be ready for flight once it achieved its freedom from the cocoon.

Sometimes struggles are exactly what we need in our life. If God allowed us to go through our life without any obstacles, it would cripple us. We would not be as strong as what we could have been.

And we could never fly.

Dear Michael,

You were determined to get your shoe tied as you left for preschool one day. I kept offering to help but you insisted that you were going to do it by yourself. An admirable trait for a four-year-old! It was very difficult to stand there and watch you struggle with those laces, trying to make a "bunny ear" with one lace and then hold it and try to do the same with the other lace.

Your frustration grew after your numerous tries. As you got more frustrated and began to cry, I felt like it was time to step in and help. As a parent, I believe our first instinct is to want to offer our assistance. We want to help; we want to take the discomfort away.

Sometimes, though, it is in everyone's best interest to let you struggle through the hard times, to experience the pain of failure or the pain of rejection. These experiences with adversity will only make you stronger.

Your mom and I are always here to help. The help might not be evident to you at first, or it may seem like we are not helping at all. But we always have your best interests at heart. (And isn't that a wonderful thought, that parents are willing to do what it takes to help!)

I love you all so much. Think then, for a moment, about God's love for you and how much more He is there to answer your needs.

I realize that at times it may be difficult to see where God's hand is in your life. Please believe that He is there, loving you more than your mind can imagine. Always have faith in Him and know that He cares for you so very much.

I love you,
Dad

Our greatest glory is not in never falling,
but in rising every time we fall.
~ CONFUCIUS

The Mountain

THERE WERE TWO warring tribes in the Andes, one that lived in the lowlands and the other high in the mountains. The mountain people invaded the Lowlanders one day, and as part of their plundering of the people, they kidnapped a baby from one of the Lowlander families and took the infant back up into the mountains.

The Lowlanders didn't know how to climb the mountain. They didn't know any of the trails that the mountain people used, and they didn't know where to find the mountain people or how to track them in the steep terrain. Even so, they sent out their best party of fighting men to climb the mountain and bring the baby home.

The men tried first one method of climbing and then another. They tried one trail and then another. After several days of effort, however, they had climbed only several hundred feet.

Feeling hopeless and helpless, the Lowlanders decided that the cause was lost, and they prepared to return to their village below. As they were packing their gear for the descent, they saw the baby's mother walking toward them. They realized that she was coming down the mountain that they hadn't figured out how to climb. And then they saw that she had the baby strapped to her back. How could that be?

One man greeted her and said, "We couldn't climb this mountain. How did you do this when we, the strongest and most able men in the village, couldn't do it?"

She shrugged her shoulders and said, "It was my baby."

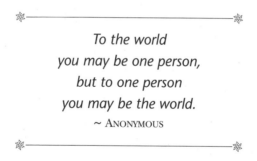

To the world
you may be one person,
but to one person
you may be the world.
~ Anonymous

Dear Christopher,

Your mom and I were awakened by your cries one night. You, being our first child and barely two weeks old, caused us great concern because you were running a very high fever in a short amount of time. We called the doctor that night and were told to immediately take you to the hospital.

The drive to the hospital, which was fifteen minutes away, seemed to take all night. We waited in the emergency room for a specialist to arrive and perform a spinal tap to see if you had spinal meningitis. As you were undergoing tests, your face turned entirely blue, and for a few seconds your mom and I thought you were dying. I stood there looking at you, praying that your face would return to its normal color. Thank God, that incident lasted only a matter of seconds before you were breathing on your own again.

We spent the next two days with you in the hospital. Mom and I took turns sleeping on a foldout chair and a regular chair. Neither of us felt like going home, so we just spent most of our time with you in the room. You were supposed to be baptized the weekend this happened. Most of our relatives had planned to come to the church and celebrate in our joy. Instead, we asked our priest to come to the hospital and baptize you there. He came and we were comforted by his presence.

It was heart-wrenching to see you hooked up to the different IVs taped around your hand. Your body, barely twenty-one inches long, only filled about an eighth of the full-size hospital bed they had put you in.

Any parent can understand the reason your mom and I stayed in close proximity to you those next few days. We didn't do it because it felt good or because we liked sleeping on chairs for a couple hours at a time. It is very simply done out of love. That's what parents do. They love you and stand by you and pray for you, all with an unconditional love. What some might not be able to understand becomes crystal clear in the eyes of a parent.

> I love you,
> Dad

Logic 101

A COLLEGE STUDENT was in a philosophy class discussing the existence of God. The professor presented the following logic:

"Has anyone in this class heard God?"

Nobody spoke.

"Has anyone in this class touched God?"

Again, nobody spoke.

"Has anyone in this class seen God?"

When nobody spoke for the third time, he simply stated, "Then there is no God."

One student thought for a second, and then asked for permission to reply. Curious to hear this bold student's response, the professor granted it, and the student stood up and asked the following questions of his classmates:

"Has anyone in this class heard our professor's brain?"

Silence.

"Has anyone in this class touched our professor's brain?"

Absolute silence.

"Has anyone in this class seen our professor's brain?"

When nobody in the class dared to speak, the student concluded, "Then, according to our professor's logic, it must be true that our professor has no brain!"

(The student received an "A" in the class.)

Dear Christopher, Michael, and Andrew,

I hope that I have been a living example that you have to believe that God is there and that he loves each of you more than your minds can ever comprehend. I have often suggested to others that if they ever doubt the existence of God, just look at the miracle of life.

When you were born, I was in total amazement as I looked at each of you for the first time. To think about all the parts of the human body, and all of yours were working perfectly. Being able to witness the gift of a human life in its first few minutes in the world is astounding. Truly, my joy at that moment was almost indescribable. The love I felt for each of you had no bounds! At that moment, I knew Heaven must exist.

How proud God must be when we are born! How much love He must feel for each of us! Know that as excited as I was to see each of you for the first time and wanted to take care of you, God is infinitely more joyous to watch over and take care of us.

I love you,
Dad

The Ticket

(for all of us in a hurry)

JACK TOOK A LONG look at his speedometer before slowing down: 73 in a 55-mile-per-hour zone. Fourth time in as many months. How could a guy get caught so often?

When his car had slowed to 10 miles an hour, Jack pulled over, but only partially. Let the cop worry about the potential traffic hazard. Maybe some other car will tweak his backside with a mirror.

The cop was stepping out of his car, the big pad in hand.

Bob? Bob from church? Jack sank farther into his trench coat. This was worse than the coming ticket. A Christian cop catching a guy from his own church. A guy who happened to be a little anxious to get home after a long day at the office. A guy he was about to play golf with tomorrow. Jumping out of the car, he approached a man he saw every Sunday, a man he'd never seen in uniform.

"Hi, Bob. Fancy meeting you like this."

"Hello, Jack." No smile.

"Guess you caught me red-handed in a rush to see my wife and kids."

"Yeah, I guess."

Bob seemed uncertain. Good. "I've seen some long days at the office lately. I'm afraid I bent the rules a bit—just this once." Jack toed at a pebble on the pavement. "Diane said something about roast beef and potatoes tonight. Know what I mean?"

"I know what you mean. I also know that you have a reputation in our precinct."

Ouch! This was not going in the right direction. Time to change tactics.

"What'd you clock me at?"

"Seventy-one. Would you sit back in your car, please?"

"Now wait a minute here, Bob. I checked as soon as I saw you. I was barely nudging 65." The lie seemed to come easier with every ticket.

"Please, Jack, in the car."

Flustered, Jack hunched himself through the still-open door. Slamming it shut, he stared at the dashboard. He was in no rush to open the window. The minutes ticked by. Bob scribbled away on the pad. Why hadn't he asked for a driver's license? Whatever the reason, it would be a month of Sundays before Jack ever sat near this cop again. A tap on the door jerked his head to the left. There was Bob, a folded paper in hand.

Jack rolled down the window a mere two inches, just enough room for Bob to pass him the slip.

"Thanks." Jack could not quite keep the sneer out of his voice.

Bob returned to his car without a word. Jack watched his retreat in the mirror. Jack unfolded the sheet of paper. How much was this one going to cost? Wait a minute. What was this? Some kind of joke? Certainly not a ticket. Jack began to read:

"Dear Jack,

Once upon a time I had a daughter. She was six when killed by a car. You guessed it—a speeding driver. A fine and three months in jail, and the man was free. Free to hug his daughters—all three of them. I only had one, and I'm going to have to wait until heaven before I can ever hug her again. A thousand times I've tried to forgive that man. A thousand times I thought I had. Maybe I did, but I need to do it again. Even now. . . . Pray for me. And be careful. My son is all I have left. Bob"

Jack twisted around in time to see Bob's car pull away and head down the road. Jack watched until it disappeared. A full fifteen minutes later, he too, pulled away and drove slowly home, praying for forgiveness and hugging a surprised wife and kids when he arrived.

Life is precious. Handle with care.

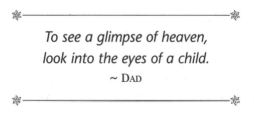

*To see a glimpse of heaven,
look into the eyes of a child.*
~ DAD

Dear Christopher, Michael, and Andrew,

I can't begin to tell you all how hearing a story of a parent losing a child makes me feel. The thought of any of you dying before me is something that I can't or won't register in my mind.

When I read in the paper about a young child dying far too young because of a careless driver or because they themselves happened to be careless, or for whatever reason, I always say a little prayer for them. The impact of such a tragic event changes the course of a parent's life forever.

When I recently read about a child who had died from an illness and saw that the family lived in our town, I decided to drive over to their house to offer my condolences. I didn't know who they were, but what I did know was that they were a parent like me. I took one of the sympathy Mass cards that I had filed away and drove over to their house.

My heart raced as I rang the doorbell and waited for someone to answer. A friend of the family came to the door, and I introduced myself and asked if I could offer my sympathy to the family. There was a house full of people because their son's wake was to be held the next day. As the mother of the young boy who had died came to greet me, I immediately got all choked up. What I could muster was that I was so sorry to hear about her son's death. It was hard for me to imagine someone so close in age to myself losing a child to leukemia.

You see, it's important to be compassionate. We don't know what effects our actions may have on other people. I regret the times that I have missed the opportunity to show compassion, but I hope that we as a family have been able to touch some lives along the way. Remember, what seems small or insignificant to the world may in fact have a profound effect on the recipient of your compassion or generosity.

You are all so precious to me. The thought of ever losing one of you is too heart wrenching to dwell on. I will do everything in my power to keep you from harm's way when we are together. I pray to God that he looks over you when I can't be with you. He has given me three irreplaceable gifts. I love each of you with all my heart and our Heavenly Father loves you infinitely more.

I love you,
Dad

A Famous Father

HE WASN'T A world leader or a famous doctor or a war hero or a sports figure. He was no business tycoon, and you will never see his name in the financial pages. But he was one of the greatest men who ever lived. He was my father.

I guess you might say he was a person who was never interested in getting credit or receiving honors. He did corny things like pay bills on time, go to church on Sunday, and serve as an officer in the P.T.A.

He helped his kids with their homework and drove his wife to do the grocery shopping on Thursday nights. He got a great kick out of hauling his teenagers and their friends to and from football games.

Tonight is my first night without him. I don't know what to do with myself. I am sorry now for the times I didn't show him the proper respect. But I am grateful for a lot of other things.

I am thankful that God let me have my father for fifteen years. And I am happy that I was able to let him know how much I loved him. That wonderful man died with a smile on his face and fulfillment in his heart. He knew that he was a great success as a husband and a father, a brother, a son, and a friend.

I wonder how many millionaires can say that.

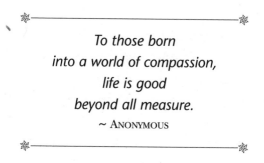

*To those born
into a world of compassion,
life is good
beyond all measure.*

~ ANONYMOUS

Dear Christopher, Michael, and Andrew,

I want to thank you for being appreciative children to me. You have told me often that you are glad I am your dad. Comments like that mean so much to me.

I'm so thankful that we get to spend a lot of time together. We are blessed to have each other.

If success was defined by money and power, there are certainly many in this world who are more successful than me. I'm glad that we can define success by the love we have for each other and by the wealth of riches we share as a family.

As part of your internal wealth, know today and every day that my love for you is something you can always count on.

Some day, when you pull this note out again, my last day on earth will have passed. Have no regrets. You have been wonderful sons and a blessing to me.

I love you,
Dad

Is Your Hut Burning?

THE ONLY SURVIVOR of a shipwreck was washed up on a small, uninhabited island. He prayed feverishly for God to rescue him, and every day he scanned the horizon for help, but none seemed forthcoming. Exhausted, he eventually managed to build a little hut out of driftwood to protect him from the elements, and to store his few possessions.

But then one day, after scavenging for food, he arrived home to find his little hut in flames, the smoke rolling up to the sky. The worst had happened; everything was lost. He was stunned with grief and anger.

"God, how could you do this to me?" he cried.

Early the next day, however, he was awakened by the sound of a ship that was approaching the island. It had come to rescue him.

How did you know I was here?" asked the weary man of his rescuers.

"We saw your smoke signal," they replied.

It is easy to get discouraged when things are going bad. But we shouldn't lose heart, because God is at work in our lives, even in the midst of pain and suffering.

Remember, the next time your little hut is burning to the ground, it just may be a smoke signal that summons the grace of God. For all the negative things we have to say to ourselves, God has a positive answer for them.

You say: It's impossible.

God says: All thing are possible (Luke 18:27).

You say: I'm too tired.

God says: I will give you rest (Matthew 11:28–20).

You say: Nobody really loves me.

God says: I love you (John 3:16 and 13:34).

You say: I can't go on.

God says: My grace is sufficient (2 Corinthians 12:9 and Psalm 91:15).

You say: I can't figure things out.

God says: I will direct your steps (Proverbs 3:5–6).

You say: I can't do it.

God says: You can do all things (Philippians 4:13).

You say: I'm not able.

God says: I am able (2 Corinthians 9:8).

You say: It's not worth it.

God says: It will be worth it (Romans 8:28).

You say: I can't forgive myself.

God says: I forgive you (1 John 1:9 and Romans 8:1).

You say: I can't manage.

God says: I will supply all your needs (Philippians 4:19).

You say: I'm afraid.

God says: I have not given you a spirit of fear (2 Timothy 1:7).

You say: I'm always worried and frustrated.

God says: Cast all your cares on me (1 Peter 5:7).

You say: I don't have enough faith.

God says: I've given everyone a measure of faith (Romans 12:3).

You say: I'm not smart enough.

God says: I give you wisdom (1 Corinthians 1:30).

You say: I feel all alone.

God says: I will never leave you or forsake you (Hebrews 13:5).

Measure wealth
not by the things you have,
but by the things you have
for which
you would not take money.
~ ANONYMOUS

Dear Christopher, Michael, and Andrew,

Recently, Mom and I took the three of you for your annual check-ups at the doctor's office. Everything was going fine until we got to Andrew. The doctor was listening to his heartbeat for what appeared to be a lot longer than what he had just done with the other two of you. As your mom and I looked at each other, the doctor turned to us and said that he would like to have a pediatric heart specialist listen to Andrew's heart. The doctor didn't think it was anything serious, but he wanted to be sure.

At that point, all kinds of thoughts went through my head. If it is not serious, why are we going to a heart specialist? What if the one percent the doctor is not sure about turns out to be something very wrong with Andrew's heart? With all these thoughts in my mind, I took a few moments to say a silent prayer to Saint Anthony, the miracle worker. What else could I do? I took the referral information from our doctor. As we left the office, all your mom and I could do was pray that Andrew's heart had only a murmur as our doctor suspected and nothing else.

At times like this, it is easy to say things like, "Why us?" "Why Andrew?" I think those are fairly normal first reactions to situations that you wish you didn't have to go through.

I found comfort in the following little story that was shared with me. A man complained that his cross was too heavy. God took him to a large room and told him to set his cross down and find one that he liked better and that He would be glad to trade with the man. The man did as God suggested. All the crosses that the man picked up seemed heavier except for one. It was the one that he had come in with.

When things aren't always going your way, when you feel your cross is too heavy, it is very important to believe and have faith that you were put in the situation for a reason and that your cross is the proper weigh for you. God doesn't close one door without opening another. He doesn't promise that we won't experience pain or suffering, but He does promise that He will be there to help us through.

Well, as you know by now, our visit to the pediatric heart specialist turned out okay. Andrew has what they call an innocent heart murmur. Your mom and I are so grateful that he is okay. We certainly trust in God and are so very thankful for his mercy.

I love you,
Dad

Dads, Beware

"DADDY, HOW MUCH do you make an hour?" With a timid voice and idolizing eyes, the little boy greeted his father as he returned from work.

Greatly surprised, but giving his boy a glaring look, the father said: "Look, sonny, not even your mother knows that. Don't bother me now, I'm tired."

"But, Daddy, just tell me, please! How much do you make an hour?" the boy insisted.

The father, finally giving up, replied: "Twenty dollars per hour."

"Okay, Daddy. Could you loan me ten dollars?" the boy asked.

Showing his restlessness and positively disturbed, the father yelled: "So that was the reason you asked how much I earn, right? Go to sleep and don't bother me anymore!"

It was already dark and the father was meditating on what he said and was feeling guilty. Maybe, he thought, his son wanted to buy something.

Finally, trying to ease his mind, the father went to his son's room. "Are you asleep, son?" asked the father.

"No, Daddy. Why?" replied the boy, partially asleep.

"Here's the money you asked for earlier," the father said.

"Thanks, Daddy!" rejoiced the son, while putting his hand under his pillow and removing some money. "Now I have enough! Now I have twenty dollars!" the boy said to his father, who was gazing at his son, confused at what his son had just said. "Daddy, could you sell me one hour of your time?"

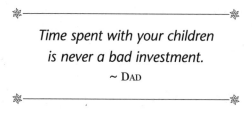

Time spent with your children
is never a bad investment.

~ DAD

Dear Christopher, Michael, and Andrew,

At this stage of my life, I am most thankful for the gift of time, especially for the time that I am able to spend with each of you. As your dad, I hope to be there for each milestone in your lives.

To be able to watch each of you move out of your crib into a bed, go off to school for the first day, or play organized sports for the first time—these were all fun things for me to be part of as I have watched you grow older by the day.

As you get older the milestones that a parent witnesses get bigger—that first full day of high school, high school proms and graduation, college graduations, and your first real job.

Once college is over, if you choose to marry, every parent loves to be there to witness the start of a new life for their child. If children are in God's plan for you, that will bring you so much joy. And it will fill us with pride and joy as well.

As we all get older with each passing day, I am continuously grateful for your presence in my life. Just being around the three of you is a blessing that I hope I have conveyed on a regular basis. I am very thankful for the title of "Father" and I find so much joy in being "Dad." I am most thankful for the gift of time with each of you.

I love you,
Dad

---

*Teach your children
to respect the title of "Father,"
and you'll have fun
just being "Dad."*

~ DAD

I Love You

I LEFT FOR WORK one evening while my two children were busy sewing things on the sewing machine. My eleven-year-old daughter was, in the midst of her project, going to assist her older brother in making a little cushion.

In a few hours I returned to find a mess in the kitchen and front room, and both children were sitting in front of the television. Having had a long day, I was very short with my greeting to them. Then I noticed the material my daughter had used. It had been purchased to make a color-coordinated baby blanket, and chunks had been cut out of almost every piece of fabric.

Not stopping to listen, I exploded at the children and explained how angry I was at what they had done. My daughter listened to me sheepishly, not trying to defend herself at all, but the pain could be seen written across her face. She retreated to her room quietly, and spent some time in there alone before she came out to say good night and once again apologize for the mistake she had made.

A few hours later, as I was preparing for bed, there on my bed lay a beautiful little cushion made out of the forbidden fabric, with the words "I LOVE MOM." Alongside it was a note apologizing again.

To this day, I still get tears in my eyes when I think of how I reacted, and I still feel the pain of my actions. It was I who then sheepishly went to her and apologized profusely for my actions. I display with great pride the cushion on my bed, and use it as a constant reminder that nothing in this world is greater than a child's love.

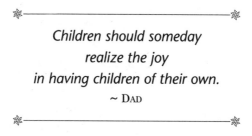

*Children should someday
realize the joy
in having children of their own.*

~ DAD

Dear Christopher, Michael, and Andrew,

The gift of children. You all deserve to have children some day. I mean that in the most loving way possible. The joy that you experience when you have children of your own is beyond emotional description. For all of you, whom I love so dearly, I hope that some day you experience the same joy that I have been able to share with the three of you.

I think Mom put it best when she shared this thought with me. She said that you think you love your parents as much as they love you. But, in fact, parents love their children at a level that is, at times, hard to comprehend. That is the way it should be. Mom and I know you love us. We love you more than you can ever imagine.

Our extended family loves you all as well. Whether it's your aunt Kristi and her family fifteen minutes away or your aunt Mary Ann or aunt Jean thousands of miles away, Mom and I always want you to know that you are surrounded by love.

As great as that love is, if you have children of your own some day, I'm sure that you will feel that love that is beyond compare. Know, too, how much our Heavenly Father loves each one of you. It is always hard for me to try and equate the love that God has for us.

I know how much I love you. I hope you always feel my love for you. Believe that God loves you so much more. Don't make it too complicated. It's rather simple. Know that He just loves you. In your darkest hour, know that He loves each of you.

Just as I have sat with each of you with my arm around your shoulder, so too does God wrap his loving arms around you in times of joy and sorrow. Don't forget to include Him in your joy, and I'm sure He will be there to comfort you in your inevitable sorrows.

It is truly a heartwarming thought to know that we are loved so deeply.

With my love,
Dad

The "Empty" Box

SOME TIME AGO a friend punished his three-year-old daughter for wasting a roll of gold wrapping paper. Money was tight, and he became infuriated when the child tried to decorate a box to put under their Christmas tree. Nevertheless, the little girl brought the gift to her father the next morning and said, "This is for you, Daddy." He was embarrassed by his earlier overreaction, but his anger flared again when he found that the box was empty.

He yelled at her, "Don't you know that when you give someone a present, there's supposed to be something inside of it?"

The little girl looked up at him with tears in her eyes and said, "Oh, Daddy, it's not empty. I blew kisses into the box. All for you, Daddy."

The father was crushed. He put his arms around his little girl, and begged her forgiveness.

My friend told me that he kept that gold box by his bed for years. Whenever he was discouraged, he would take out an imaginary kiss and remember the love of the child who had put it there.

In a very real sense, each of us as parents has been given a gold container filled with unconditional love and kisses from our children. No more precious possession could anyone hold.

Life is not measured
by the breaths we take
but by the moments
that take our breath away.

~ ANONYMOUS

Dear Christopher,

Today at the bus stop you paused to say "I love you." You said it without reservation, in front of all your peers. I want you to know how much that means to me.

I know the time will come when I will be dropping you off two blocks from your final destination because that's what teenagers do. But the time now is worth every moment. You are a true joy to have as my son. Days like this I will forever remember.

Time marches on and, in the not-too-distant future, you won't be that seven-year old looking back at me telling me that you love me as you board the bus. I know that love will still be there, but there is something special about a seven-year-old communicating the emotion of love so unconditionally.

Today I put that "I love you" in my own imaginary box and I will carry it with me wherever I go. I want you to always know that moments like that mean the world to me, and at moments like that I thank God I'm alive.

                                        I love you,
                                        Dad

Dear Michael,

Tonight we had Dads' Night at your preschool. It was such a joy to spend that special time with you, just the two of us. It always makes me so happy that you are proud to bring me into your classroom and let me share in nights like this. I am proud to call you my son. I will always treasure the picture of you and me and the letter holder that we made together that night.

You are a good son to me, and I love the times that we share together.

I love you,
Dad

*D*ear Andrew,

 Today after your nap, when you looked at me with the eyes of a child just waking up and told me that you "love Daddy," my heart swelled with love as I thought to myself that life doesn't get much better than this. It's at times like this that my outlook and attitude can change for the better in a matter of seconds, and I realize how lucky I am to be a dad.

 I want you to know that as I grow older, the hugs and the "I love you's" that you share with me are something that I will long remember.

I love you,
Dad

Saturday Morning

THE OLDER I GET, the more I enjoy Saturday mornings. Perhaps it's the quiet solitude that comes with being the first to rise, or maybe it's the unbounded joy of not having to be at work. Either way, the first few hours of a Saturday morning are most enjoyable.

A few weeks ago, I was shuffling toward the kitchen with a steaming cup of coffee in one hand and the morning paper in the other. What began as a typical Saturday morning turned into one of those lessons that life seems to hand you from time to time. Let me tell you about it.

I turned the volume up on my radio to listen to a Saturday morning talk show. I heard an older sounding chap with a golden voice. You know the kind. He sounded like he should be in the broadcasting business himself. He was talking about "a thousand marbles" to someone named "Tom."

I was intrigued and sat down to listen to what he had to say. "Well, Tom, it sure sounds like you're busy with your job. I'm sure they pay you well, but it's a shame you have to be away from home and your family so much. Hard to believe a young fellow should have to work sixty or seventy hours a week to make ends meet. Too bad you missed your daughter's dance recital."

He continued, "Let me tell you something, Tom, something that has helped me keep a good perspective on my own priorities." And then he explained his theory of a "thousand marbles."

"You see, I sat down one day and did a little arithmetic. The average person lives about seventy-five years. I know, some live more and some live less, but on average, folks live about seventy-five years.

"Now, then, I multiplied seventy-five times fifty-two, and I came up with thirty-nine hundred, which is the number of Saturdays that the average person has in their entire lifetime. Now, stick with me, Tom. I'm getting to the important part.

"It took me until I was fifty-five years old to think about all this in any detail," he went on, "and by that time I had lived through over twenty-eight hundred Saturdays. I got to thinking that if I lived to be seventy-five, I only had about a thousand of them left to enjoy. So I went to a toy store and bought every single marble they had. I ended up having to visit three toy stores to round up a thousand marbles. I took them home and put them inside a large, clear plastic container right here in my workshop next to the radio. Every Saturday since then, I have taken one marble out and thrown it away.

"I found that by watching the marbles diminish, I focused more on the really important things in life. There is nothing like watching your time here on this earth run out to help get your priorities straight.

"Now, let me tell you one last thing before I sign off with you and take my lovely wife out for breakfast. This morning, I took the very last marble out of the container. I figure if I make it until next Saturday, then I have been given a little extra time. And the one thing we can all use is a little more time.

"It was nice to talk to you, Tom, I hope you spend more time with your loved ones, and I hope to meet you again someday. Have a good morning!"

You could have heard a pin drop when he finished. Even the show's moderator didn't have anything to say for a few moments. I guess he gave us all a lot to think about. I had planned to do some work that morning, then go to the gym. Instead, I went upstairs and woke my wife up with a kiss. "C'mon, honey, I'm taking you and the kids to breakfast."

"What brought this on?" she asked with a smile.

"Oh, nothing special. It's just been a long time since we spent a Saturday together with the kids. Hey, can we stop at a toy store while we're out? I need to buy some marbles."

Dear Christopher, Michael, and Andrew,

We sure do love Saturdays. This particular Saturday we were going to climb the dirt hill across the street at the construction site. It was a little cold out so we put on an extra layer of clothes.

The four of us headed over to the hill while Mom went to work at the store. We had a great time, didn't we? Climbing up those hills that were higher than our rooftop made you guys feel like you were real mountain climbers. We slid down the steep side as if we were skiing, only to end up down at the bottom covered in dirt.

Friends of yours that happened to be riding by said that had to be one of the funnest things to do. They said that you were lucky that we had taken the time to climb the hill together. To me, that's being a dad in its simplest and purest form. It is not power, wealth, or fame that should bring you true joy in this life. It's family. It's being a good person, a good son, a good husband, a good father.

When it came time to leave and we ran back home, you guys had just as much fun taking your dirty clothes off in the garage and standing there in your underwear.

A morning like this didn't cost us a cent, but to me it is worth a fortune. I can't imagine a better way for me to spend my time than to be with the three of you. I love who we are when we're together.

Thanks for enjoying the simple things in our life.

                love,

                Dad

---

*There are many ways
to measure success;
not the least of which
is the way your child
describes you to a friend.*

~ ANONYMOUS

Tomorrow

IF I KNEW this would be the last time that I'd see you fall
asleep,
I would tuck you in more tightly and pray the Lord your soul
to keep.
If I knew this would be the last time that I'd see you walk out
the door,
I would give you a hug and a kiss and call you back for one
more.
If I knew this would be the last time I'd hear your voice lifted
up in praise,
I would videotape each action and word, so I could play
them back day after day.
If I knew this would be the last time, I could spare an extra
minute or two
to stop and say "I love you," instead of assuming you would
know I do.
If I knew this was to be the last day I would be there to share
with you,
well, I'm sure you'll have so many more, so I can let just this
one slip away.

For surely there is always tomorrow to make up for an
   oversight,
and we always get a second chance to make everything right.
There will always be another day to say our "I love you's."
And certainly there's to be another chance to say our
   "Anything I can do's?"
But just in case I might be wrong, and today is all I get,
I'd like to say how much I love you and I hope we never
   forget.
Tomorrow is not promised to anyone, young or old alike,
and today may be the last chance you get to hold your loved
   one tight.
So if you're waiting for tomorrow, why not do it today?
For if tomorrow never comes, you'll surely regret the day
that you didn't take that extra time for a smile, a hug, or
   a kiss,
and you were too busy to grant someone
what turned out to be their one last wish.
So hold your loved ones close today, and whisper in their ear.
Tell them how much you love them and that you'll always
   hold them dear.
Take time to say "I'm sorry." "Please forgive me." "Thank
   you." or "It's okay."
And if tomorrow never comes, you'll have no regrets
   about today.

Dear Christopher, Michael, and Andrew,

Time sure does march on, and I pray that the three of you have an appreciation for that as you grow older. Just the other day I was talking with your grandpa about how long it has been since my own grandfather had passed away.

It has been over thirty years since that Sunday afternoon when my parents came home from the hospital to say that my grandfather had passed away. I remember it like yesterday, lying on the floor, covering my face with my small hands to hide the tears.

As I look back, there are things that I wished as an eight-year old that I was able to do with him before he died. There are things I wished I had said.

I remember going with my dad and my grandmother to the cemetery years after my grandfather had passed away, watching my grandmother cry over his grave. Even at that young age, it is something that leaves an unforgettable impression. You can feel the love they must have had for each other. Now, you almost ache for them and the sorrow they felt at that time.

One thing that always stuck with me, even as a young boy, is how my dad took care of his own mother after his dad died. He didn't wait for someone else to do it; he didn't wait until tomorrow to get things done.

Although we are a young family now, look after Mom as she gets older. Also, look after and care for each other. You are brothers, and you will find that to be one of your best gifts in life. It doesn't take too much time to call Mom or each other to see how everyone else is doing, to say "Thanks" or "I love you."

I want each of you to know how much I love you, today and every day. I want to say "Thank you" for being fine sons to me and Mom. If my life were to end tomorrow, I want you to know that God has truly blessed me with the gift of each of you. I realize that we are not promised tomorrow, although I hope we see many more of them. So, today, know that my love for you knows no bounds, know that I am proud to call you "Son."

I love you,
Dad

The Cab Ride

TWENTY YEARS AGO, I drove a cab for a living. It was a cowboy's life, a life for someone who wanted no boss. What I didn't realize was that it was also a ministry. Because I drove the night shift, my cab became a moving confessional. Passengers climbed in, sat behind me in total anonymity, and told me about their lives.

I encountered people whose lives amazed me, ennobled me, made me laugh and weep. But none touched me more than a woman I picked up late one August night.

I was responding to a call from a small brick fourplex in a quiet part of town. I assumed I was being sent to pick up some partygoers, or someone who had just had a fight with a lover, or a worker heading to an early shift at some factory in the industrial part of town.

When I arrived at 2:30 a.m., the building was dark except for a single light in a ground-floor window. Under these circumstances, many drivers would just honk once or twice, wait a minute, then drive away. But I had seen too many impoverished people who depended on taxis as their only means of transportation. Unless a situation smelled of danger, I always went to the door. *This passenger might be someone who needs my assistance,* I reasoned to myself.

So I walked to the door and knocked.

"Just a minute," answered a frail, elderly voice.

I could hear something being dragged across the floor. After a long pause, the door opened. A small woman in her eighties stood before me. She was wearing a print dress and a pillbox hat with a veil pinned on it, like somebody out of a 1940s movie. By her side was a small nylon suitcase. The apartment looked as if no one had lived in it for years. All the furniture was covered with sheets. There were no clocks on the walls, no knickknacks or utensils on the counters. In the corner was a cardboard box filled with photos and glassware.

"Would you carry my bag out to the car?" she asked.

I took the suitcase to the cab, then returned to assist the woman. She took my arm and we walked slowly toward the curb. She kept thanking me for my kindness.

"It's nothing," I told her. "I just try to treat my passengers the way I would want my mother to be treated."

"Oh, you're such a good boy," she said. When we got in the cab, she gave me an address and then asked, "Could you drive through downtown?"

"It's not the shortest way," I answered quickly.

"Oh, I don't mind," she said. "I'm in no hurry. I'm on my way to a hospice."

I looked in the rearview mirror. Her eyes were glistening.

"I don't have any family left," she continued. "The doctor says I don't have very long."

I quietly reached over and shut off the meter. "What route would you like me to take?" I asked.

For the next two hours, we drove through the city. She showed me the building where she had once worked as an elevator operator. We drove through the neighborhood where she and her husband had lived when they were newlyweds. She had me pull up in front of a furniture warehouse that had once been a ballroom where she had gone dancing as a girl. Sometimes she'd ask me to slow in front of a particular building or corner and would sit staring into the darkness, saying nothing.

As the first hint of sun was creasing the horizon, she suddenly said, "I'm tired. Let's go now."

We drove in silence to the address she had given me. It was a low building, like a small convalescent home, with a driveway that passed under a portico. Two orderlies came out to the cab as soon as we pulled up. They were solicitous and intent, watching her every move. They must have been expecting her.

I opened the trunk and took the small suitcase to the door. The woman was already seated in a wheelchair. "How much do I owe you?" she asked, reaching into her purse.

"Nothing," I said.

"You have to make a living," she answered.

"There are other passengers," I responded. Almost without thinking, I bent and gave her a hug. She held on to me tightly.

"You gave an old woman a little moment of joy," she said. "Thank you."

I squeezed her hand and then walked into the dim morning light. Behind me, a door shut. It was the sound of the closing of a life.

I didn't pick up any more passengers that shift. I drove aimlessly, lost in thought. For the rest of that day, I could hardly talk. What if that woman had gotten an angry driver, or one who was impatient to end his shift? What if I had refused to take the run, or had honked once, and then driven away?

On a quick review, I don't think that I have done anything more important in my life. We're conditioned to think that our lives revolve around great moments. But great moments often catch us unaware—beautifully wrapped in what others may consider a small one.

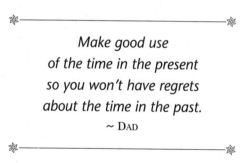

*Make good use
of the time in the present
so you won't have regrets
about the time in the past.*

~ DAD

WILLIAM JOHNSON

Dear Christopher, Michael, and Andrew,

We went to church today, the same as every Sunday. After church we went to visit some of the elderly in our parish, people who cannot physically get to the church anymore. We visited three residents at the Wingler House. They were all delighted to see us, especially the three of you. The residents really enjoy seeing you guys (at least in small doses).

By the time we were through with our visit, Ms. Mary had told us about her days in New York and how they visited other family members on Sundays. Mr. Andy was a little sad today as he talked about how he had moved into this two-bedroom condo that he and his wife were going to share. She never moved in with him. She died of cancer two months before the move.

And finally, Mr. Charles and Ms. Mary told us about the nine children that they had been blessed with, but also about the sadness that sometimes comes with being a parent. One of their sons, in his early forties, had died of cancer four months earlier, leaving behind a wife and young child. Mr. Charles and Ms. Mary, although very sad from what they experienced, have accepted it as part of God's overall plan in their lives, a wonderful example of faith.

Listen and be compassionate—you'll find that to be one special way people become attracted to you. Ask questions and listen to what they have to say. It is easy to talk and tell everyone about yourself. It is much harder to listen. One of the best ways to leave others with a good feeling, a feeling of self-worth, is to listen to them.

Too often we underestimate the power of a touch, a smile, an ear to listen with, a kind word, a truly heartfelt compliment, or a small act of caring. These, in all honesty, aren't going to change the world, but they might have a positive impact on someone's life.

People may not remember exactly what you did or what you said, but they will always remember how you made them feel.

God has given each of us 86,400 seconds in our day. How many of them are you willing to spend so that others might see you as caring and compassionate?

Remember, you can live an extraordinary life by doing ordinary things.

love,
Dad

The Empty Egg

JEREMY WAS BORN with a twisted body and a slow mind. At the age of twelve he was still in second grade, seemingly unable to learn. His teacher, Doris Miller, often became exasperated with him. He would squirm in his seat, drool, and make grunting noises. At other times, he spoke clearly and distinctly, as if a spot of light had penetrated the darkness of his brain. Most of the time, however, Jeremy just irritated his teacher.

One day she called his parents and asked them to come in for a consultation. As the Forresters entered the empty classroom, Doris said to them, "Jeremy really belongs in a special school. It isn't fair to him to be with younger children who don't have learning problems. Why, there is a five-year gap between his age and that of the other students."

Mrs. Forrester cried softly into a tissue while her husband spoke. "Miss Miller," he said, "there is no school of that kind nearby. It would be a terrible shock for Jeremy if we had to take him out of this school. We know he really likes it here."

Doris sat for a long time after they had left, staring at the snow outside the window. Its coldness seemed to seep into her soul. She wanted to sympathize with the Forresters. After all, their only child had a terminal illness. But it wasn't fair to keep him in her class. She had eighteen other youngsters to teach, and Jeremy was a distraction. Furthermore, he would never learn to read and write. Why waste any more time trying?

As she pondered the situation, guilt washed over her. *Here I am complaining when my problems are nothing compared to that poor family,* she thought. Lord, *please help me to be more patient with Jeremy.*

From that day on, she tried hard to ignore Jeremy's noises and his blank stares. Then one day, he limped to her desk, dragging his bad leg behind him. "I love you, Miss Miller," he exclaimed, loud enough for the whole class to hear. The other students snickered, and Doris's face burned red. She stammered, "Wh-why, that's very nice, Jeremy. N-now, please take your seat."

Spring came, and the children talked excitedly about the coming of Easter. Doris told them the story of Jesus, and then to emphasize the idea of new life springing forth, she gave each of the children a large plastic egg. "Now," she said to them, "I want you to take this home and bring it back tomorrow with something inside that shows new life. Do you understand?"

"Yes, Miss Miller," the children responded enthusiastically—all except for Jeremy. He listened intently; his eyes never left her face. He did not even make his usual noises. Had he understood what she had said about Jesus' death and resurrection? Did he understand the assignment? Perhaps she should call his parents and explain the project to them.

That evening, Doris's kitchen sink stopped up. She called the landlord and waited an hour for him to come by and unclog it. After that, she still had to shop for groceries, iron a blouse, and prepare a vocabulary test for the next day. She completely forgot about phoning Jeremy's parents.

The next morning, nineteen children came to school, laughing and talking as they placed their eggs in the large wicker basket on Miss Miller's desk. After they completed their math lesson, it was time to open the eggs. In the first egg, Doris found a flower. "Oh yes, a flower is certainly a sign of new life," she said. "When plants peek through the ground, we know that spring is here." A small girl in the first row waved her arm. "That's my egg, Miss Miller," she called out.

The next egg contained a plastic butterfly, which looked very real. Doris held it up. "We all know that a caterpillar changes and grows into a beautiful butterfly. Yes, that's new life, too." Little Judy smiled proudly and said, "Miss Miller, that one is mine."

Next, Doris found a rock with moss on it. She explained that moss, too, showed life. Billy spoke up from the back of the classroom, "My daddy helped me," he beamed.

Then Doris opened the fourth egg. She gasped. The egg was empty. Surely it must be Jeremy's she thought, and of course, he did not understand her instructions. If only she had not forgotten to phone his parents.

Because she did not want to embarrass him, she quietly set the egg aside and reached for another. Suddenly, Jeremy spoke up. "Miss Miller, aren't you going to talk about my egg?" Flustered, Doris replied, "But Jeremy, your egg is empty." He looked into her eyes and said softly, "Yes, but Jesus' tomb was empty, too."

Time stopped. When she could speak again, Doris asked him, "Do you know why the tomb was empty?"

"Oh, yes," Jeremy said, "Jesus was killed and put in there. Then His Father raised Him up."

The recess bell rang. While the children excitedly ran out to the schoolyard, Doris cried. The cold inside her melted completely away.

Three months later, Jeremy died. Those who paid their respects at the mortuary were surprised to see nineteen eggs on top of his casket . . . all of them empty.

When God measures a man,
He puts the tape around his heart
instead of his head.

~ ANONYMOUS

Dear Christopher, Michael, and Andrew,

It was a beautiful day to be off from school. Here it was, Monday, and we were going to spend the day as a family instead of each going in our own direction. We decided last night that we were going to leave the house early in the morning and drive into the city to see some of the sights.

It was Presidents' day, so you guys really wanted to go see the Lincoln Memorial, along with a stop at the White House and one of the government buildings that houses the aquarium. After visiting the aquarium, we had lunch across the street at the Ronald Reagan building. Later, on our walk over to the Lincoln Memorial, we saw a homeless man walking along Constitution Avenue.

Christopher, you asked if you could give the man some money. As you were handing him a dollar, he touched you on the shoulder, and along with his thank-you, he had this to add: "There are a lot of people who pass me on the street that wouldn't give me the time of day. Thank you for stopping, and always believe that the good Lord will take care of needs; not your wants, but your needs." What a remarkable message from an unlikely source.

That gentleman reminded me of a story your grandmother told me about my great-grandmother who died before I was born. She had no formal education—in fact, she never learned to read or write. However, she passed along much wisdom. In her gentle and loving way, she would always remind someone who was troubled to "Do your best and God will do the rest." How many times have we heard this? How simple it seems, but so very true.

Never slough off those who appear different from you. Don't ridicule or ignore them. You never know what message they bring. You don't know what's in their heart. What does it take to listen to them? Why not offer them help if you have the opportunity? Look for God in others. He created all of us. Offering help to others with no expectations in return can be a most rewarding experience.

love,
Dad

WILLIAM JOHNSON

If you want to touch the past,
touch a rock.
If you want to touch the present,
touch a rose.
If you want to touch the future,
touch a life.

~ ANONYMOUS

Each Day Is a Gift

ONE DAY, WHEN I was a freshman in high school, I saw a kid from my class walking home from school. His name was Kyle. It looked like he was carrying all of his books. I thought to myself, *Why would anyone bring home all his books on a Friday? He must really be a nerd.* I had quite a weekend planned (parties and a football game with my friends the following afternoon), so I shrugged my shoulders and went on.

As I was walking, I saw a bunch of kids running toward him. They ran at him, knocking all his books out of his arms and tripping him so he landed in the dirt. His glasses went flying, and I saw them land in the grass about ten feet from him. He looked up, and I saw this terrible sadness in his eyes. My heart went out to him. So I jogged over to him, and as he crawled around looking for his glasses, I saw a tear in his eye.

As I handed him his glasses, I said, "Those guys are jerks. They really should get lives." He looked at me and said, "Hey, thanks!" There was a big smile on his face.

It was one of those smiles that showed real gratitude. I helped him pick up his books, and asked him where he lived. As it turned out, he lived near me, so I asked him why I had never seen him before. He said he had transferred from a private school. I would have never hung out with a private school kid before.

We talked all the way home, and I carried his books. He turned out to be a pretty cool kid. I asked him if he wanted to play football on Saturday with me and my friends. He said yes.

We hung out all weekend and the more I got to know Kyle, the more I liked him. And my friends thought the same of him. Monday morning came, and there was Kyle with the huge stack of books again. I stopped him and said, "Darn, boy, you're gonna build some serious muscles with this pile of books every day!" He just laughed and handed me half the books.

Over the next four years, Kyle and I became best friends. When we were seniors, we began to think about college. Kyle decided on Georgetown, and I was going to Duke. I knew that we would always be friends, that the miles would never be a problem. He was going to be a doctor, and I was going for business on a football scholarship.

Kyle was valedictorian of our class. I teased him all the time about being a nerd. He had to prepare a speech for graduation. I was so glad it wasn't me having to get up there and speak.

Graduation day, Kyle looked great. He was one of those guys who really found himself during high school. He filled out and actually looked good in glasses. He had more dates than me, and all the girls loved him! Boy, sometimes I was jealous! Today was one of those days.

I could see that Kyle was nervous about his speech. So I smacked him on the back and said, "Hey, big guy, you'll be great!" He looked at me with one of those looks (the really grateful one) and smiled. "Thanks," he said.

As he started his speech, he cleared his throat, and began. "Graduation is a time to thank those who helped you make it through those tough years. Your parents, your teachers, your siblings, maybe a coach, but mostly your friends. I am here to tell all of you that being a friend to someone is the best gift you can give them. I am going to tell you a story."

I just looked at my friend with disbelief as he told the story of the first day we met. He had planned to kill himself over the weekend. He talked of how he had cleaned out his locker so his mom wouldn't have to do it later and was carrying his stuff home. He looked hard at me and gave me a little smile. "Thankfully, I was saved. My friend saved me from doing the unspeakable."

I heard the gasp go through the crowd as this handsome, popular boy told us all about his weakest moment. I saw his mom and dad looking at me and smiling that same grateful smile. Not until that moment did I realize its depth.

Never underestimate the power of your actions. With one small gesture you can change a person's life. Each day is a gift from God! Don't forget to say "Thank you!"

Dear Christopher,

Today after school you told Mom and me about one of your friends at school. After lunch you were walking back to your classroom when you saw a kid you shared a classroom with the previous year. He was walking down to lunch. One of the children in your class who knew Frank yelled across the hallway that Frank wasn't very smart and a few of the other kids in line started to laugh. You simply said to the kid in your class that was teasing him, "So." As you know, Frank was held back a year, and he was still in first grade while the rest of you had gone on to the second grade. We are proud of you for sticking up for someone else. It is certainly not always easy to do, especially when you are the smallest kid in the class.

Don't give up who you are to please others or to be like them. Continue to be concerned with those who have less than you or for those who can't, or won't, speak for themselves. Take care of those who are less fortunate than yourself. You never know what affect your small act of kindness might have on someone's life. Always try to be charitable in word and action.

Love,
Dad

❋ ————————————————————————— ❋

You have not lived
until you have done something
for someone who
can never repay you.
~ ANONYMOUS

❋ ————————————————————————— ❋

The Brown Paper Bag

(A true story of Robert Fulghum
and his seven-year-old daughter Molly)

IT WAS MOLLY'S job to hand her father his brown paper lunch bag each morning before he headed off to work. One morning, in addition to his usual lunch bag, Molly handed him a second paper bag. This one was worn and held together with duct tape, staples, and paper clips.

"Why two bags?" Fulghum asked.

"The other is something else," Molly answered.

"What's in it?"

"Just some stuff. Take it with you."

Not wanting to hold court over the matter, Fulghum stuffed both sacks into his briefcase, kissed Molly, and rushed off. At midday, while hurriedly scarfing down his real lunch, he tore open Molly's bag and shook out the contents: two hair ribbons, three small stones, a plastic dinosaur, a pencil stub, a tiny sea shell, two animal crackers, a marble, a used lipstick, a small doll, two chocolate kisses, and thirteen pennies.

Fulghum smiled, finished eating, and swept the desk clean—into the wastebasket—leftover lunch, Molly's junk, and all.

That evening, Molly ran up behind him as he read the paper.

"Where's my bag?"

"What bag?"

"You know, the one I gave you this morning."

"I left it at the office. Why?"

"I forgot to put this note in it," she said. "And, besides, those are my things in the sack, Daddy, the ones I really like—I thought you might like to play with them, but now I want them back. You didn't lose the bag, did you, Daddy?"

"Oh, no," he said, lying. "I just forgot to bring it home. I'll bring it tomorrow."

While Molly hugged her father's neck, he unfolded the note that had not made it into the sack: "I love you, Daddy."

Molly had given him her treasures. All that a seven-year-old held dear. Love in a paper sack, and he missed it—not only missed it, but had thrown it in the wastebasket. So back he went to the office. Just ahead of the night janitor, he picked up the wastebasket and poured the contents on his desk.

After washing the mustard off the dinosaurs and spraying the whole thing with breath freshener to kill the smell of onions, he carefully smoothed out the wadded ball of brown paper, put the treasures inside, and carried it home gingerly, like an injured kitten. The bag didn't look so good, but the stuff was all there and that's what counted.

After dinner, he asked Molly to tell him about the stuff in the sack. It took a long time to tell. Everything had a story or a memory or was attached to dreams and imaginary friends. Fairies had brought some of the things. He had given her the chocolate kisses, and she had kept them for when she needed them.

"Sometimes I think of all the times in this sweet life," Fulghum concludes the story, "when I must have missed the affection I was being given."

We should all remember that it's not the destination that counts in life, it's the journey. The little-girl smiles, the dinosaurs and chocolate kisses wrapped in old paper bags that we sometimes throw away too thoughtlessly, each day, each a tiny treasure."

The journey with the people we love is all that really matters. Such a simple truth so easily forgotten.

Dear Boys,

The journey so far with the three of you and Mom has been wonderful. Sometimes I am literally amazed at how much God has blessed us by getting to spend so much time with each other.

Being able to do all the little, simple things that we do together is such a joy. I want you to know how much fun Mom and I have with you when we can all go fishing together, take a ride to the local store for a fifteen-cent popsicle (yes, there are still some things out there for fifteen cents), or just hang around the yard and play baseball. These are the things I love about being your dad. These are the things that I don't want to miss out on now and regret later on.

I enjoy the chance to come to your school, Christopher, and have lunch with you. I love the opportunity to take Michael to school, and I always look forward to being with Andrew around the house.

All the little projects that the three of you have helped me with—painting the walls, washing the car, cutting the grass, and even baking Mom's birthday cake—are memories that are most dear to me.

The unexpected hugs or the "I love you" for no reason at all, these are the things that bring me real joy. I'm so glad that I'm able to experience all your love and affection. Just being with you has made my life so complete. I hope you all know the joy I get from just being your dad and being able to call the three of you my sons.

>I love you,
>Dad

---

*Don't get caught standing
knee-deep in your child's love
dying of loneliness.*
~ DAD

The Missed Gift

A YOUNG MAN was getting ready to graduate from college. For many months he had admired a beautiful sports car in a dealer's showroom, and knowing his father could well afford it, he told him that was all he wanted.

As graduation day approached, the young man awaited signs that his father had purchased the car. Finally, on the morning of his graduation, his father called him into his private study. His father told him how proud he was to have such a fine son, and told him how much he loved him. He handed his son a beautifully wrapped gift box.

Curious, and somewhat disappointed, the young man opened the box and found a lovely, leather-bound Bible, with the young man's name embossed in gold. Angry, he raised his voice to his father and said, "With all your money, you give me a Bible?" and stormed out of the house.

Many years passed and the young man was very successful in business. He had a beautiful home and a wonderful family, but he realized his father was very old, and thought perhaps he should go to him. He had not seen him since that graduation day.

Before he could make arrangements, he received a telegram telling him his father had passed away and had willed all of his possessions to his son. He needed to come home immediately and take care of things.

When he arrived at his father's house, sudden sadness and regret filled his heart. He began to search through his father's important papers and saw the still gift-wrapped Bible, just as he had left it years ago. With tears, he opened the Bible and began to turn the pages. His father had carefully underlined a verse, Matthew 7:11: "And if ye, being evil, know how to give good gifts to your children, how much more shall your Father which is in heaven give to those who ask Him?"

As he read those words, a car key dropped from the back of the Bible. It had a tag with the dealer's name, the same dealer who had the sports car he had desired. On the tag was the date of his graduation, and the words PAID IN FULL.

Please don't miss God's blessings because you can't see past your own desires.

Dear Christopher, Michael, and Andrew,

Sometimes you ask for something that your mom and I don't give to you. At this stage of your life, it might be hard for you to understand why you can't have something. You might even do what a lot of kids your age do and keep asking until you finally think you are going to get it.

Know that we always hear you and that your requests are answered. It might not be the answer that you are looking for, but we try to do what we feel is best for you at the time. Many times your mom and I see the bigger picture and we know that whatever you want might not be good for you at that time or perhaps we just can't afford it.

It is not shameful to have less than "they" have. We believe that you will appreciate things more if you have to work for them yourselves. Too often we confuse our "needs" with our "wants."

Think of the fun we have when we make sailboats out of cardboard, or go fishing with sticks and some string. Times like that have cost us barely a cent, but they are times that are worth a fortune.

You'll find that some of the best things in life aren't about how much money you have but about how much love you possess. Many of my best times are simply spent with each of you. We could be taking a bike ride, throwing the ball in the backyard, reading a book, or just hanging out together. Times like these are most memorable to me.

Mom and I love you more than you could ever imagine. God loves you infinitely more, and He will be there to take care of your needs.

I love you,
Dad

I used to complain
because I had no shoes,
then one day I met a man
who had no feet.

~ ANONYMOUS

Gilbert's Ride

MY SON GILBERT was eight years old and had been in Cub Scouts only a short time. During one of his meetings he was handed a sheet of paper, a block of wood, and four tires, and told to return home and give it all to "dad."

That was not an easy task for Gilbert to do. Dad was not receptive to doing things with his son. But Gilbert tried. Dad read the paper and scoffed at the idea of making a pinewood derby car with his young, eager son.

The block of wood remained untouched as the weeks passed. Finally, Mom stepped in to see if she could figure this all out. The project began. Having no carpentry skills, I decided it would be best if I simply read the directions and let Gilbert do the work. And he did. I read aloud the measurements, the rules of what they could and couldn't do.

Within days his block of wood was turning into a pinewood derby car. A little lopsided, but looking great (at least through the eyes of Mom). Gilbert had not seen any of the other kids' cars and was feeling pretty proud of his "Blue

Lightning," the pride that comes with knowing you did something on your own.

Then the big night came. With his blue pinewood derby car in his hand and pride in his heart, we headed to the big race. Once there my little one's pride turned to humility. Gilbert's car was obviously the only car made entirely on his own. All the other cars were a father-son partnership, with cool paint jobs and sleek body styles made for speed.

A few of the boys giggled as they looked at Gilbert's lopsided, wobbly, unattractive vehicle. To add to the humility, Gilbert was the only boy without a man at his side. A couple of the boys who were from single-parent homes at least had an uncle or grandfather by their side. Gilbert had "Mom."

As the race began it was done in elimination fashion. You kept racing as long as you were the winner. One by one the cars raced down the finely sanded ramp. Finally, it was between Gilbert and the sleekest, fastest-looking car there. As the last race was about to begin, my wide-eyed, shy, eight-year-old asked if they could stop the race for a minute, because he wanted to pray.

The race stopped.

Gilbert hit his knees clutching his funny looking block of wood between his hands. With a wrinkled brow he set to converse with his Father. He prayed in earnest for a very long minute and a half. Then he stood, smile on his face, and announced, "Okay, I am ready."

As the crowd cheered, a boy named Tommy stood with his father as their car sped down the ramp. Gilbert stood with his Father within his heart and watched his block of wood wobble down the ramp with surprising speed and rush over the finish line a fraction of a second before Tommy's car.

Gilbert leaped into the air with a loud thank-you as the crowd roared in approval. The Scout Master came up to Gilbert with microphone in hand and asked the obvious question: "So you prayed to win, huh, Gilbert?" To which my young son answered, "Oh, no, sir. That wouldn't be fair to ask God to help you beat someone else. I just asked Him to make it so I don't cry when I lose."

Children seem to have a wisdom far beyond us. Gilbert didn't ask God to win the race; he didn't ask God to fix the outcome. Gilbert asked God to give him strength in the outcome. When Gilbert first saw the other cars he didn't cry out to God, "No fair; they had a father's help." No, he went to his Father for strength.

Perhaps we spend too much of our prayer time asking God to rig the race, to make us number one, or too much time asking God to remove us from the struggle, when we should be seeking God's strength to get through the struggle. "I can do everything through Him who gives me strength" (Philippians 4:13).

Gilbert's simple prayer spoke volumes to those present that night. He never doubted that God would indeed answer his request. He didn't pray to win, and thus hurt someone else. He prayed that God would supply the grace to lose with dignity. Gilbert, by stopping the race to speak to his Father, also showed the crowd that he wasn't there without a "dad," but his Father was most definitely there with him. Yes, Gilbert walked away a winner that night, with his Father at his side.

To one who has faith,
no explanation is necessary.
To one without faith,
no explanation is possible.
~ SAINT THOMAS AQUINAS

Dear Christopher, Michael, and Andrew,

Please be mindful that things aren't always going to go the way that you had planned. Understand, though, that like your mother and I hope to protect you and give you the things you need, God understands your needs far greater than you can imagine.

When my position was eliminated, I had received enough "thanks, but no thanks" from potential employers to last me a lifetime. But I knew if I persevered, if I listened and prayed, He would answer. You have a choice. You can look to the past or move on to the future. Choose to channel your energy into something positive. Rarely can we control what others say or do. However, you can control your reaction to someone's response.

I like to believe that I know, for the most part, what you need. Now, it may not always be what you want, but that's okay. How could God not know what we need? I must admit that, at times, I have said to God, "Okay, this is what I need."

Well, you know what? As time passed, it wasn't what I needed at all. It's what I thought I needed. My unanswered prayer was in fact the answer. Combine hard work with faith and every situation will work out for the best.

Your grandmother shared this story with me. A man had complained to God about the length of his cross. He said to God, "Why can't this cross be shorter so that it wouldn't be so heavy?" God agreed to cut off a piece. The man continued his travels. An enemy approached and the man hurried away. He came to a chasm and on the other side was freedom. The only way across was to lay down his cross over the opening and hope it reached to the other side so that he could walk across. He tried to lay his cross down but found that it was too short by the amount that he had asked God to cut off.

God is more interested in making us what He wants us to be than in giving us what we think we ought to have. Although we may not understand difficulties that come our way, pray for the strength and courage to be able to handle a situation and to be able to deal with the outcome.

Remember, don't waste too much of your energy trying to kick down the door that has been closed. Rather, gently crawl through the open window of opportunity.

I love you,
Dad

Timeless Love

MY GRANDPARENTS were married for over half a century and played their own special game from the time they met each other.

The goal of their game was to write the word "shmily" in a surprise place for the other to find. They took turns leaving "shmily" around the house. As soon as one of them discovered it, it was their turn to hide it once more. They dragged "shmily" with their fingers through the sugar and flour containers to await whoever was preparing the next meal.

They smeared it in the dew on the windows overlooking the patio where my grandma always fed us warm, homemade pudding with blue food coloring. "Shmily" was written in the steam left on the mirror after a hot shower, where it would reappear bath after bath. At one point, my grandmother even unrolled an entire roll of toilet paper to leave "shmily" on the very last sheet. There was no end to the places "shmily" would pop up. Little notes with "shmily" scribbled hurriedly were found on dashboards and car seats, or taped to steering wheels.

The notes were stuffed inside shoes and left under pillows. "Shmily" was written in the dust upon the mantel and traced in the ashes of the fireplace.

This mysterious word was as much a part of my grand-parents' house as the furniture. It took me a long time before I was able to fully appreciate my grandparents' game.

Skepticism has kept me from believing in true love—one that is pure and enduring. However, I never doubted my grandparents' relationship. They had love down pat. It was more than their flirtatious little games; it was a way of life. Their relationship was based on a devotion and passionate affection, which not everyone is lucky enough to experience. Grandma and Grandpa held hands every chance they could.

They stole kisses as they bumped into each other in their tiny kitchen. They finished each other's sentences and shared the daily crossword puzzle and word jumble. My grandma whispered to me about how cute my grandpa was, how handsome and old he had grown to be. She claimed that she really knew "how to pick 'em." Before every meal they bowed their heads and gave thanks, marveling at their blessings: a wonderful family, good fortune, and each other. But there was a dark cloud in my grandparents' life: my grandmother had breast cancer.

The disease had first appeared ten years earlier. As always, Grandpa was with her every step of the way. He comforted her in their yellow room, painted that way so that she could always be surrounded by sunshine, even when she was too sick to go outside.

Now the cancer was again attacking her body. With the help of a cane and my grandfather's steady hand, they went to church every Sunday morning. But my grandmother grew steadily weaker until finally she could not leave the house anymore.

For a while, Grandpa would go to church alone, praying to God to watch over his wife. Then one day, what we all dreaded finally happened. Grandma was gone.

"Shmily" was scrawled in yellow on the pink ribbons of my grandmother's funeral bouquet. As the crowd thinned and the last mourners turned to leave, my aunts, uncles, cousins, and other family members came forward and gathered around Grandma one last time.

Grandpa stepped up to my grandmother's casket and, taking a shaky breath, he began to sing to her. Through his tears and grief, the song came, a deep and throaty lullaby. Shaking with my own sorrow, I will never forget that moment. For I knew that, although I couldn't begin to fathom the depth of their love, I had been privileged to witness its unmatched beauty.

S-H-M-I-L-Y: See How Much I Love You.

Dear Christopher, Michael, and Andrew,

One of the best things that I can do for you as your father is to love Mom. I hope that I have showed you my love for her in the way that I treat her on a daily basis. She has been, and continues to be, a real blessing in my life. She is a wonderful wife to me and a wonderful mother to the three of you.

I hope I live long enough to see Mom's blonde hair turn gray, to be at her side through the years, to let her know that I still care. I hope to always be there for her, as I said on our wedding day, till death do us part. I have always considered our marriage a love story. A story that I hope will endure, somehow, into eternity.

Mom is never too busy to play with you, read to you, or pray with you. She is always there to spend time with you. She really appreciates the time you guys spend together.

I look forward to so many more years with you and Mom. Your mom and I have talked about how we look forward to growing old together and watching you guys grow. We look forward to watching all three of you go through the different milestones in your lives: graduations, career choices, and possibly marriage and children of your own.

One day, when my work here on earth ends, I will die, but believe that I am not dead. Hopefully, in God's infinite mercy, I will be with Him, waiting for the rest of you. As I eagerly wait for each of you to come home and spend time with me, so too does our Heavenly Father long for us to come to our eternal home and be with Him. I like to think that someday we will all be together forever.

It's hard for me to think about my life here without any of you. I pray that God watches over all of us. It is a privilege to be your father and to be able to call the three of you my sons. I am proud that I can share in your lives.

I love you,
Dad

Don't cry because it's over;
smile because it happened.
~ ANONYMOUS

Busy Hands

MY HANDS WERE busy through the day,
I didn't have much time to play
The little games you asked me to.
I didn't have much time for you.
I'd wash your clothes, I'd sew and cook,
But when you'd bring your picture book
And ask me please to share your fun,
I'd say: "A little later, son."
I'd tuck you in all safe at night
And hear your prayers, turn out the light,
Then tiptoe softly to the door . . .
I wish I'd stayed a minute more.
For time is short, the years rush past.
A little boy grows up so fast.
No longer is he at your side,
His precious secrets to confide.
The picture books are put away;
There are no longer games to play,
No good-night kiss, no prayers to hear . . .

That all belongs to yesteryear.
My hands, once busy, now are still.
The days are long and hard to fill.
I wish I could go back and do
The little things you asked me to.

*Regret only the things that your children
would not say about you with love,
once you are gone.*

~ DAD

Dear Boys,

I have tried to use this as a guide to keep me from regretting the years as you get older that I didn't do enough with you when you were young.

I heard a song on the radio today about a daughter who never really got to know her dad because he was always busy doing other things. She calls him the greatest man she never knew. I have never wanted that to be the case with me. I want you to know who I am and how I feel about each of you. I want you to always feel the love that I have for you.

You are the three most important people to Mom and me. The times that you had to be disciplined for whatever reason have been, I hope, far outweighed by the times that I have told each of you how much I love you.

I hope that you will keep these letters long after I am gone. I want you to always know that you have been nothing but a joy in my life. My only wish each day is to be able to spend at least one more day with all of you.

I have been blessed to realize that the gift of time moves all too quickly and that my years with you are relatively short. I cherish the time we are able to spend together. I pray that my regrets are few.

I love you,
Dad

Where Is God's Perfection?

IN BROOKLYN, New York, Chush is a school that caters to learning-disabled children. Some children remain in Chush for their entire school career, while others can be mainstreamed into conventional schools.

At a Chush fund-raising dinner, the father of a Chush child delivered a speech that would never be forgotten by those who attended. After extolling the school and its dedicated staff, he cried out, "Where is the perfection in my son Shaya? Everything God does is done with perfection. But my child cannot understand things as other children do. My child cannot remember facts and figures as other children do. Where is God's perfection?"

The audience was shocked by the question, pained by the father's anguish, and stilled by the piercing query. "I believe," the father answered, "that when God brings a child like this into the world, the perfection that he seeks is in the way people react to this child." He then told the following story about his son Shaya:

One afternoon Shaya and his father walked past a park where some older boys Shaya knew were playing baseball. Shaya asked, "Do you think they will let me play?" Shaya's father knew that his son was not at all athletic and that most boys would not want him on their team. But he understood that if his son was chosen to play it would give him a comfortable sense of belonging.

Shaya's father approached one of the boys in the field and asked if Shaya could play. The boy looked around for guidance from his teammates. Getting none, he took matters into his own hands and said, "We are losing by six runs and the game is in the eighth inning. I guess he can be on our team and we'll try to put him up to bat in the ninth." Shaya's father was ecstatic as Shaya smiled broadly.

Shaya was told to put on a glove and go out to play short center field. In the bottom of the eighth inning, Shaya's team scored a few runs but was still behind by three. In the bottom of the ninth inning, Shaya's team scored again and now with two outs and the bases loaded with the potential winning run on base, Shaya was scheduled to be up.

Would the team actually let Shaya bat at this juncture and give away their chance to win the game? Surprisingly, Shaya was given the bat.

Everyone knew that it was all but impossible because Shaya didn't even know how to hold the bat properly, let alone hit with it. However, as Shaya stepped up to the plate, the pitcher moved in a few steps to lob the ball in softly so Shaya should at least be able to make contact. The first pitch came in and Shaya swung clumsily and missed. One of

Shaya's teammates came up to Shaya and together they held the bat and faced the pitcher waiting for the next pitch.

The pitcher again took a few more steps forward to toss the ball softly toward Shaya. As the pitch came in, Shaya and his teammate swung at the bat and together they hit a slow ground ball to the pitcher. The pitcher picked up the soft grounder and could easily have thrown the ball to the first baseman. Shaya would have been out and that would have ended the game. Instead, the pitcher took the ball and threw it beyond reach of the first baseman. Everyone started yelling, "Shaya, run to first. Run to first."

Never in his life had Shaya run to first base. He scampered down the baseline wide-eyed and startled. By the time he reached first base, the right fielder had the ball. He could have thrown the ball to the second baseman who would tag out Shaya, who was still running. But the right fielder understood the pitcher's intentions, so he threw the ball high and far over the second baseman's head as everyone cheered on Shaya. Shaya ran toward second base as the runners ahead of him circled the bases toward home.

As Shaya reached second base, he didn't know where next to run. Amazingly, the opposing short stop ran to him, turned him in the direction of third base, and loudly encouraged, "Run to third."

As Shaya rounded third, the boys from both teams ran behind him happily yelling, "Shaya, run home." Shaya ran home, stepped on home plate, and all eighteen boys formed a mass; two lifted him on their shoulders and made him the hero, as he had just hit a "grand slam" and won the game for his team.

"That day," said the father softly with tears now rolling down his face, "those eighteen boys reached their level of God's perfection."

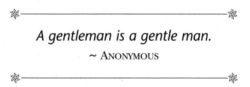

A gentleman is a gentle man.

~ ANONYMOUS

Dear Christopher, Michael, and Andrew,

Be compassionate. The things you do that may not seem very important to you may mean the world to someone else. Be kind and considerate of those who appear different from you. Visit the sick. Visit the elderly. Pay your respects to the deceased and to their families.

Treat everyone with politeness, even those who might not be polite to you. Do it not because they are gentlemen, but because you are. Show people that there is a lot of good in the world. Try to give others the benefit of good judgment. Err on the side of mercy.

Think of others as you live your life. I know it can be easy to shut others out because we seem to get too busy with our own lives. Remember, though, that it really doesn't take a whole lot of effort to make someone else feel God's love in their life. At moments like that, when we can show others that there is so much good in the world, we have, at some level, reached God's perfection.

I love you,
Dad

Dad is Driving

A SPEAKER ONCE shared this experience:

While he and his family were in Europe, it happened that they needed to drive three days continuously, day and night, to get to Germany. So, they all got into the car—he, his wife, and his three-year-old daughter. His little daughter had never traveled at night before. She was scared the first night in the car with the deep darkness outside.

"Where are we going, Daddy?"

"To your uncle's house, in Germany."

"Have you been to his house before?"

"No."

"Then, do you know the way?"

"Maybe, we can read the map."

Short pause. "Do you know how to read the map?"

"Yes, we will get there safely."

Another pause. "Where are we going to eat if we get hungry before we arrive?"

"We can stop by restaurants if we are hungry."

"Do you know if there are restaurants on the way?"

"Yes, there are."

"Do you know where?"

"No, but we will be able to find some."

The same dialogue repeated a few times the first night, and again the second night. But on the third night, his daughter was quiet. The speaker thought that she might have fallen asleep, but when he looked into the mirror, he saw that she was awake and was just looking around calmly. He couldn't help wondering why she was not asking the questions anymore.

"Dear, do you know where we are going?"

"Germany, Uncle's house."

"Do you know how we are getting there?"

"No."

"Then why aren't you asking anymore?"

"Because Daddy is driving."

"Because Daddy is driving." This answer from a three-year-old girl has become the strength and help for this speaker for the many years following whenever he has questions and fears on his journey with the Lord. Yes, our Father is driving. We may know the destination (and sometimes we may just know it like the little girl— "Germany"—without understanding where or what it really is). We do not know the way, we do not know how to read the map, we do not know if we can find restaurants along the way. But the little girl knew the most important thing— Daddy is driving—and so she felt safe and secure. She knew that her daddy would provide all that she needed.

Do you know that your Daddy, the Great Shepherd, is driving today? What is your response as a passenger, His child?

You may have asked many questions before, but can you realize, like the little girl, that the most important focus should be, "Daddy is driving."

A person never stands so tall
as when they get down
on their knees to pray.
~ ANONYMOUS

Dear Christopher, Michael, and Andrew,

Today, as we were driving in the car, one of you asked me, "How is it that dads always seem to know where to go?" I explained that we learn to follow the road signs and that maps are useful guides for us.

Your question also has a much bigger meaning as well. When it comes to things in life, I don't always know where to go. When things don't go my way or when I lose my patience or when one of you is emotionally hurt by a friend or has an illness that required medical attention, I am not always sure what to do. But we always find the way. That way is usually through perseverance and faith.

The one constant in all these situations has been prayer, and a belief that as much as I want to take care of you and figure out what is best, our good Lord knows the path that we should be on. He is always there to help us. If it is God's will, He will make it so. He is our Heavenly "Dad" and we should always be comforted in the fact that He knows where He wants to take us.

One of my favorite Bible readings is from the Gospel of John. "Do not let your hearts be troubled. Trust in God; trust also in me. In my Father's house are many rooms; if it were not so, I would have told you. I am going there to prepare a place for you." Believe it! He is preparing a place for you. He knows where we are going.

As you like to see your friends each day, think of Jesus as your friend. Know that he longs to hear from you each day. He wants you to visit with Him. Nothing pleases Him more than to have a conversation with each of you. Pray and listen and you will always be at peace. Travel life's roads together with Him and he will lead you home.

I love you,
Dad

On God's Watch

A COLD MARCH wind danced around the dead of night in Dallas as the doctor walked into the small hospital room of Diana Blessing. Still groggy from surgery, she held the hand of her husband David as they braced themselves for the latest news.

That afternoon of March 10, 1991, complications had forced Diana, only twenty-four weeks pregnant, to undergo an emergency caesarean to deliver the couple's new daughter, Danae Lu Blessing. At twelve inches long and weighing only one pound, nine ounces, they already knew she was perilously premature. Still, the doctor's soft words dropped like bombs. "I don't think she's going to make it," he said as kindly as he could. "There's only a ten percent chance she will live through the night, and even then, if by some slim chance she does make it, her future could be a very cruel one."

Numb with disbelief, David and Diana listened as the doctor described the devastating problems Danae would likely face if she survived. She would never walk. She would never talk. She would probably be blind. She would certainly be prone to other catastrophic conditions, from cerebral palsy to complete mental retardation. And on and on.

"No! No!" was all Diana could say. She and David, with their five-year-old son Dustin, had long dreamed of the day they would have a daughter and become a family of four. Now, within a matter of hours, that dream was slipping away.

Through the dark hours of morning as Danae held onto life by the thinnest thread, Diana slipped in and out of drugged sleep, growing more and more determined that their tiny daughter would live—and live to be a healthy, happy young girl. But David, fully awake and listening to additional dire details of their daughter's chances of ever leaving the hospital alive, much less healthy, knew he must confront his wife with the inevitable.

"David walked in and said that we needed to talk about making funeral arrangements," Diana remembers. "I felt so bad for him because he was doing everything, trying to include me in what was going on, but I just wouldn't listen. I couldn't listen."

I said, "No. That is not going to happen. No way! I don't care what the doctors say, Danae is not going to die! One day she will be just fine, and she will be coming home with us!"

As if willed to live by Diana's determination, Danae clung to life hour after hour, with the help of every medical machine and marvel her miniature body could endure. But as those first days passed, a new agony set in for David and Diana.

Because Danae's underdeveloped nervous system was essentially "raw," the lightest kiss or caress only intensified her discomfort—so they couldn't even cradle their tiny baby girl against their chests to offer the strength of their love. All they could do, as Danae struggled alone beneath the ultraviolet light in the tangle of tubes and wires, was pray that God would stay close to their precious little girl.

There was never a moment when Danae suddenly grew stronger. But as the weeks went by, she did slowly gain an ounce of weight here and an ounce of strength there.

At last, when Danae turned two months old, her parents were able to hold her in their arms for the very first time. And two months later—though doctors continued to gently but grimly warn that her chances of surviving, much less living any kind of normal life, were next to zero—Danae went home from the hospital, just as her mother had predicted.

Today, five years later, Danae is a petite but feisty young girl with glittering gray eyes and an unquenchable zest for life. She shows no signs, whatsoever, of mental or physical impairments.

Simply, she is everything a little girl can be and more—but that happy ending is far from the end of her story.

One blistering afternoon in the summer of 1996 near her home in Irving, Texas, Danae was sitting in her mother's lap in the bleachers of a local ball park where her brother Dustin's baseball team was practicing. As always, Danae was chattering nonstop with her mother and several other adults sitting nearby when she suddenly fell silent.

Hugging her arms across her chest, Danae asked, "Do you smell that?"

Smelling the air and detecting the approach of a thunderstorm, Diana replied, "Yes, it smells like rain."

Danae closed her eyes and again asked, "Do you smell that?"

Once again, her mother replied, "Yes, I think we're about to get wet. It smells like rain."

Still caught in the moment, Danae shook her head, patted her thin shoulders with her small hands and loudly announced, "No, it smells like Him. It smells like God when you lay your head on His chest."

Tears blurred Diana's eyes as Danae then happily hopped down to play with the other children before the rains came her daughter's words confirmed what Diana and all the members of the extended Blessing family had known, at least in their hearts, all along.

During those long days and nights of the first two months of her life, when her nerves were too sensitive for them to touch her, God was holding Danae on His chest—and it is His loving scent that she remembers so well.

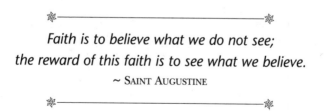

Faith is to believe what we do not see;
the reward of this faith is to see what we believe.
~ SAINT AUGUSTINE

Dear Christopher, Michael, and Andrew,

Your cousin Molly died today. She died before she had a chance to be born. Your aunt Patti was only four months pregnant. I often wonder why God sent her to our family for such a brief period of time.

He, in his infinite wisdom, gave Molly the gift of life for a few precious months. I certainly believe that she is an angel for all of us and that she is someone who can help us as we continue our journey to our eternal home.

Although it is a very sad time for Aunt Patti and Uncle Rich, their faith and trust in God is helping them. I hope, when the inevitable sadness, challenges, or obstacles occur in your life, you will look to the Father with faith and trust. Know that He is there, waiting to hear from you, ready to help.

I love you,
Dad

The Man in the Glass

WHEN YOU GET what you want in your struggle for self
And the world makes you king for a day,
Just go to a mirror and look at yourself
And see what that man has to say.
For it isn't your father or mother or wife
Whose judgment upon you must pass,
The fellow whose verdict counts most in your life
Is the one staring back from the glass.
Some people might think you're a straight-shootin' guy
And call you a wonderful guy.
But the man in the glass says you're only a bum
If you can't look him straight in the eye.
He's the fellow to please, never mind all the rest
For he's with you clear to the end.
And you've passed your most dangerous test
If the guy in the glass is your friend.
You may fool the whole world down the pathway of years
And get pats on the back as you pass,
But your final reward will be heartache and tears
If you've cheated the man in the glass.

Dear Christopher, Michael, and Andrew,

When all is said and done, the things you do in your life ultimately come down to this: can you look at yourself in the mirror and be happy with the person looking back at you? Are you satisfied with your character, doing the right thing when no one else is looking?

Many people will walk in and out of your life. Choose your paths wisely. Know that the footprints of mine and Mom's love will forever be in your hearts. Know that the unconditional love we have for you will forever be in ours.

With the ever-guiding hand of God above, as the three of you "look in the mirror" of your life, I pray that you will be happy with the reflection looking back.

I love you,
Dad

*If you're headed in the wrong direction,
God allows U-turns.*

~ ANONYMOUS

Rules, Cheap Gifts, Laughter, and Signs on the Highway to Heaven

Rules for Kids

1. My hands are small. Please don't expect perfection whenever I make a bed, draw a picture, or throw a ball. My legs are short. Please slow down so that I can keep up with you.

2. My eyes have not seen the world as yours have. Please let me explore safely. Don't restrict me unnecessarily.

3. Housework will always be there. I'm only little for such a short time. Please take time to explain things to me about this wonderful world, and do so willingly.

4. My feelings are tender. Please be sensitive to my needs. Don't nag me all day long. (You wouldn't want to be nagged for your inquisitiveness.) Treat me as you would like to be treated.

5. I am a special gift from God. Please treasure me, holding me accountable for my actions, giving me guidelines to live by, and disciplining me in a loving manner.

6. I need your encouragement and your praise to grow. Please go easy on the criticism. Remember, you can criticize the things I do without criticizing me.

7. Please give me the freedom to make decisions concerning myself. Permit me to fail so that I can learn from my mistakes. Then someday, I'll be prepared to make the kinds of decisions life requires of me.

8. Please don't do things over for me. Somehow that makes me feel that my efforts didn't quite measure up to your expectations. I know it's hard, but please don't compare me with my brother or my sister.

9. Please don't be afraid to leave for a weekend together. Kids need vacations from parents, just as parents need vacations from kids. Besides, it's a great way to show us kids that your marriage is very special.

10. Please take me to worship regularly, setting a good example for me to follow.

Cheap Gifts— Eight Gifts that Do Not Cost a Cent

THE GIFT OF LISTENING . . .
But you must REALLY listen. No interrupting, no daydreaming, no planning your response. Just listening.

THE GIFT OF AFFECTION . . .
Be generous with appropriate hugs, kisses, pats on the back, and holds. Let these small actions demonstrate the love you have for family and friends.

THE GIFT OF LAUGHTER . . .
Clip cartoons. Share articles and funny stories. Your gift will say, "I love to laugh with you."

THE GIFT OF A WRITTEN NOTE . . .
It can be a simple "Thanks for the help" note or a full sonnet. A brief, handwritten note may be remembered for a lifetime, and may even change a life.

THE GIFT OF A COMPLIMENT . . .
A simple and sincere "You look great in red," "You did a super job," or "That was a wonderful meal" can make someone's day.

THE GIFT OF A FAVOR . . .
Every day, go out of your way to do something kind.

THE GIFT OF SOLITUDE . . .
There are times when we want nothing more than to be left alone. Be sensitive to those times and give the gift of solitude to others.

THE GIFT OF A CHEERFUL DISPOSITION . . .
The easiest way to feel good is to extend a kind word to someone. Really it's not that hard to say, "Hello" or "Thank you."

Remember to Laugh—
Children's Letters to God

Dear GOD,

Instead of letting people die and having to make new ones, why don't You just keep the ones You have? —Jane

Dear GOD,

Maybe Cain and Abel would not kill each other so much if they had their own rooms. It works with my brother. —Larry

Dear GOD,

If You watch me in church on Sunday, I'll show You my new shoes. —Mickey

Dear GOD,

In school they told us what You do. Who does it when You are on vacation? —Jane

Dear GOD,

Did You mean for the giraffe to look like that or was it an accident? —Norma

Dear GOD,

Is it true my father won't get into Heaven if he uses his bowling words in the house? —Anita

Dear GOD,

Who draws the lines around the countries? —Nan

Dear GOD,

I went to this wedding and they kissed right in church. Is that okay? —Neil

Dear GOD,

What does it mean You are a Jealous God? I thought You had everything. —Jane

Dear GOD,

It rained for our whole vacation and is my father mad! He said some things about You that people are not supposed to say, but I hope You will not hurt him anyway. —Your friend (But I am not going to tell You who I am)

Dear GOD,

My brother told me about being born but it doesn't sound right. They're just kidding, aren't they? —Marsha

Dear GOD,

I would like to live 900 years like the guy in the Bible. —Love, Chris

Signs on the Highway to Heaven

(As seen on church signs throughout the country)

God promised a safe landing, not smooth sailing.

Children brought up in the church are seldom brought up in court.

Worry looks around. Faith looks up.

God doesn't need great men, great men need God.

If you stand for nothing, you'll fall for anything.

A lot of kneeling will keep you in good standing.

When it comes to giving, some people stop at nothing.

Don't have anything to be thankful for, check your pulse.

Children need models, not critics.

Aspire to inspire before you expire.

Satan can't bring you down any further than your knees.

Give God what's right, not what's left.

Don't wait for six strong men to carry you into church.

A man who can kneel before God can stand up to anything.

If you pause to think, you will have cause to thank.

If you were on trial for being a Christian,
would there be enough evidence to convict you?

Dear Christopher, Michael, and Andrew,

I hope your mom and I have done our best to follow the "Rules."

I hope we have given you enough "Cheap Gifts" to last a lifetime.

I hope the laughter has been something you will long remember.

I hope the "signs" help keep you pointed in the right direction.

I consider all of you a blessing in my life. You have changed my life for the better in ways that I could have never imagined. I consider my greatest accomplishment in life the privilege of raising the three of you and being your dad.

Together Forever.

I love you all,
Dad

The best things in life aren't things at all.
~ ANONYMOUS

---

*"In the end,
each of us will be judged
by our standard of life,
not by our standard of living,
by our measure of giving,
not by our measure of wealth;
by our simple goodness,
not by our seeming greatness."*

~ UNKNOWN

If you would like to submit a "letter of love," written to someone in your family for possible future publication, please do so by contacting me by e-mail at:

billj@storiesfromtheheart.com

Or you may visit my website at:

www.storiesfromtheheart.com

Thank you for your interest and support.